Teaching Little Fingers To Play More

by

Leigh Kaplan

A follow-up book to
Teaching Little Fingers to Play

Follows the John Thompson Tradition
Strengthens the skills learned in **Teaching Little Fingers to Play**
Eases the transition into the **Modern Course, First Grade Book**

Illustrations by Nick Gressle

Edited by David Engle

11995E

Note to Parents

The purpose of this book is to strengthen the skills introduced in John Thompson's *Teaching Little Fingers to Play*, thereby making the transition to the *First Grade Book* a comfortable one. Lyrics have been added to most of the pieces and they should be read before beginning the musical study. Guidelines accompany each piece, and it will be helpful if these are reviewed by parent and student together.

A most beneficial habit is for the parent to listen to the child perform his or her pieces at least once a week. This should be a regular occurrence where the parent's sole activity is attentive listening. The benefits to the child, both musical and emotional, cannot be overestimated.

To the Teacher

The purpose of this book is to strengthen the skills introduced in John Thompson's *Teaching Little Fingers to Play*, thereby making the transition to the *First Grade Book* a comfortable one.

Mr. Thompson's approach is to have the student gain considerable facility with both hands in a five-finger position before proceeding to other positions and techniques. Rather than introducing new concepts, *Teaching Little Fingers To Play More,* applies Mr. Thompson's approach to new pieces. Both hands stay in the five-finger positions, but new juxtapositions are added. Half steps are used occasionally, requiring that a finger play more than one key. Some easy two-note chords (also called harmonic intervals) are introduced, thus preparing the student for their more challenging use in the *First Grade Book*.

In *Teaching Little Fingers To Play More,* all previously learned terms, principles and techniques are employed in new contexts in order to reinforce skills. Generally the pieces are longer than those in *Teaching Little Fingers to Play*, thereby furthering concentration and stamina.

Please note that there is less fingering indicated than in *Teaching Little Fingers to Play*, thereby encouraging the student to read by note and / or interval.

Best wishes to both student and teacher for a wonderful musical adventure in *Teaching Little Fingers to Play More*!

Teaching Little Fingers To Play More

Contents

©MCMXCVII by The Willis Music Company
International Copyright Secured
Printed in the USA

4

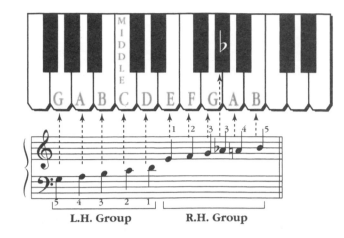

L.H. Group   R.H. Group

What is the one accidental that we find in this piece?
D.C. al Fine is the abbreviation for the Italian words *Da Capo al Fine*, which mean to return to the beginning (*Capo*) and stop at the *Fine* (end).

The Swing

♩=85 / ♩=105

Poem by Robert Louis Stevenson

Smoothly

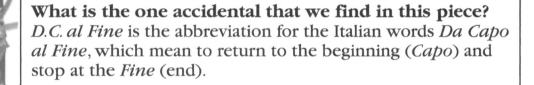

How do you like to go up in a swing?
Till I look down on the gar - den green,

5

Up in the air so blue.
Down on the roof so brown.

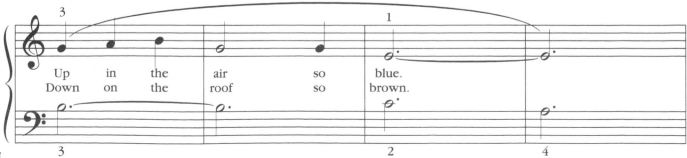

3   2   4

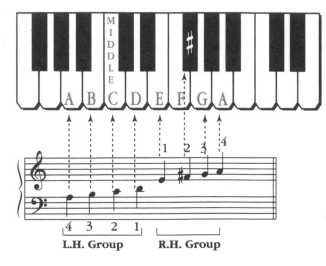

L.H. Group   **R.H. Group**

PREPARATION – Practice clapping these two rhythms as you count aloud: 𝟑/𝟒 ♩ ♩ | ♩ ♩ | and | ♩ ♩ | ♩ ♩ ||

How many F-Sharps are there in this piece? _____

Are there any F-Naturals? _____

Comin' Through the Rye 3/4 2

♩=87 / ♩=107

Medium speed

Scottish Folk Song

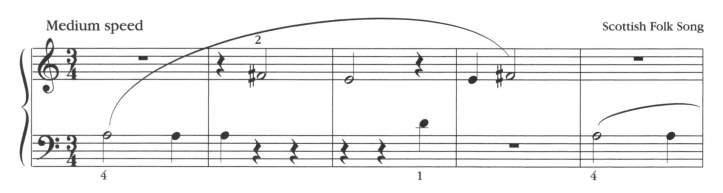

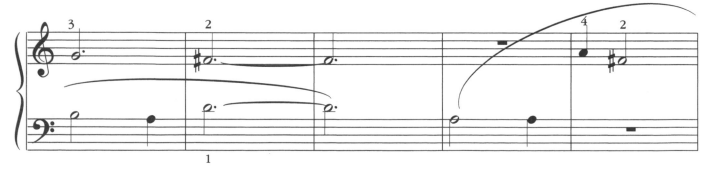

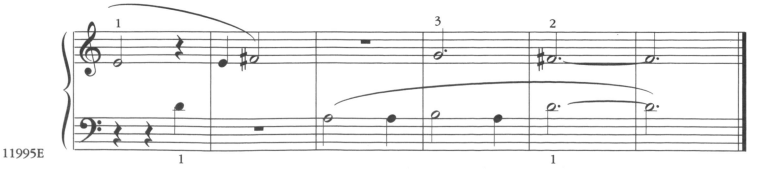

The Pet Parade

Remember that the time value of an eighth note ♪ is half as long as that of a quarter note.

An eighth rest ⅞ receives half a count, just like an eighth note.

Marchingly
medium loud

You'll see a cat, for sure a dog,

may - be a fish, per - haps a frog.

But best of all the pets you see

will be Mc - Kee, my chim - pan - zee!

11995E

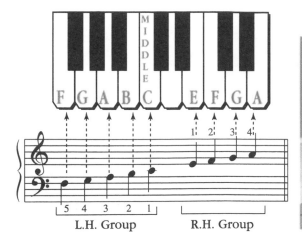

L.H. Group   R.H. Group

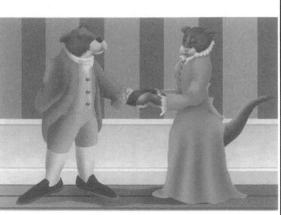

MELODY – The melody is the most important element in music.

In this piece the left hand plays the melody and the right hand plays the **accompaniment**.

Which hand should be playing louder? _____

An accent $>$ means to give extra stress.

Shall We Waltz?

7/8   4

$\quad$ =80 / =100

Glidingly

Come dance with me. Just count to three,

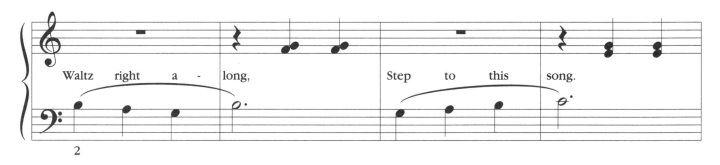

Waltz right a - long, Step to this song.

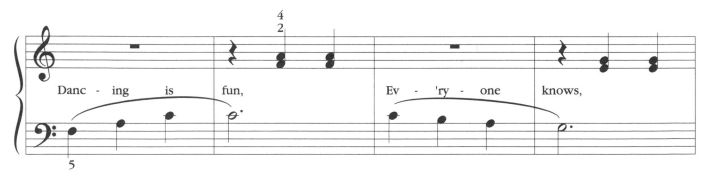

Danc - ing is fun, Ev - 'ry - one knows,

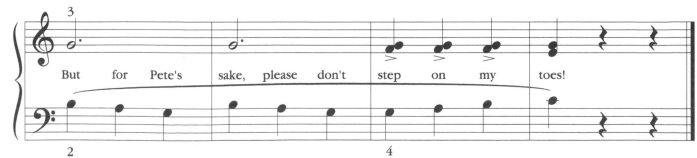

But for Pete's sake, please don't step on my toes!

11995E

To be contrary means to take an opposite point of view. In music, when one voice goes in the opposite direction of another, it is called contrary motion. How many times does the right hand make a contrary response to the left hand? _____

What do two friends in this piece finally agree upon? _____

In which measure does this happen? _____

L.H. Group   R.H. Group

On The Contrary

Medium fast

If I say "red," then you say "green." If I say "nice," then you say

"mean." If I say "fall," then you say "spring." We don't a - gree on an - y -

thing! If you say "big," then I say "small." If you say "short," then I say

getting slower

"tall." It's ver - y hard for me to see why I like you and you like me!

11995E

L.H. Group   R.H. Group

In this piece the left hand has many
B-flats and B-naturals.
How many times does the natural sign ♮
cancel the B-flat that is in the key signature?

The Top

11/12   6
♩=75 / ♩=95

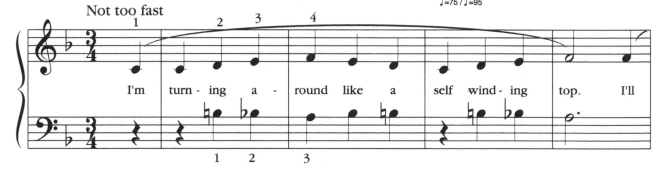

Not too fast

I'm turn - ing a - round like a self wind - ing top. I'll

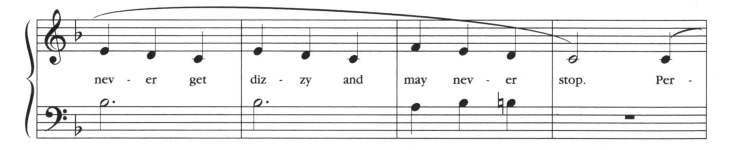

nev - er get diz - zy and may nev - er stop. Per -

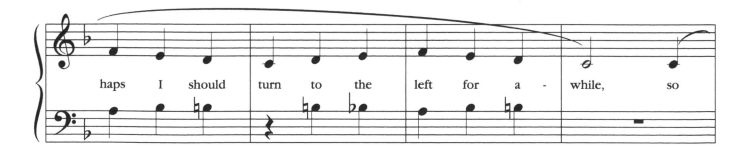

haps I should turn to the left for a - while, so

you can ad - mire my mag - ni - fi - cent style. (Ker - plop!)

11995E

The natural sign in measures 3, 5, 11 and 13 is not necessary, but it serves to remind us that the bar line has cancelled the written-in accidental in the previous measure.

Halloween Fest

♩=80 / ♩=100

Spookily

softly The witch- es and war- locks are don- ning their best,

grand- ly pre- par- ing for Hal- low- een Fest! The

gob- lins and grem- lins are quite bus- y, too,

gath- er- ing spi- ders for Hal- low- een stew!

How many measures of this piece does the left hand 'shadow' (play the same melody as) the right hand? _____

How many beats after the right hand does the left hand come in? _____

This technique of composition is called imitation. In a canon or round the imitation continues throughout the piece.

Have you ever sung a round with your friends? _____

My Shadow

15/16   8

♩=98 / ♩=118

Adapted from the poem
by Robert Louis Stevenson

Medium fast

softly

I have a lit-tle shad-ow that goes in and out with me, and

what can be the use of him is more than I can see. He's

ver - y, ver - y like me from my heels up to my head, and I

see him jump be - fore me when I jump in - to my bed.

Shad - ow, shad - ow, what can you do? For

once please be o - ri - gi - nal, so I can fol - low you.

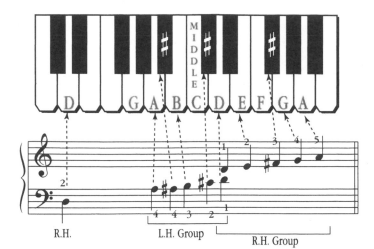

Name the sharps in PAT, MY CAT. _____ , _____ , _____ .
Where does the opening melody return? Measure _____
For how many measures is it exactly like the beginning? _____

Remember that measure number one is always the first complete measure.

Pat, My Cat

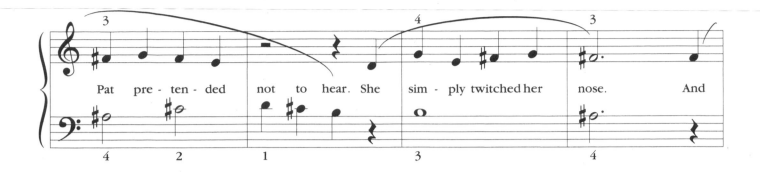

Pat pre - ten - ded not to hear. She sim - ply twitched her nose. And

then she slow - ly blinked her eyes and struck a pret - ty pose! Now,

yes, I sure did like that hat, but Pat she liked it too! And since

I like Pat, that sil - ly cat, just guess where my hat's at! *R.H. over*

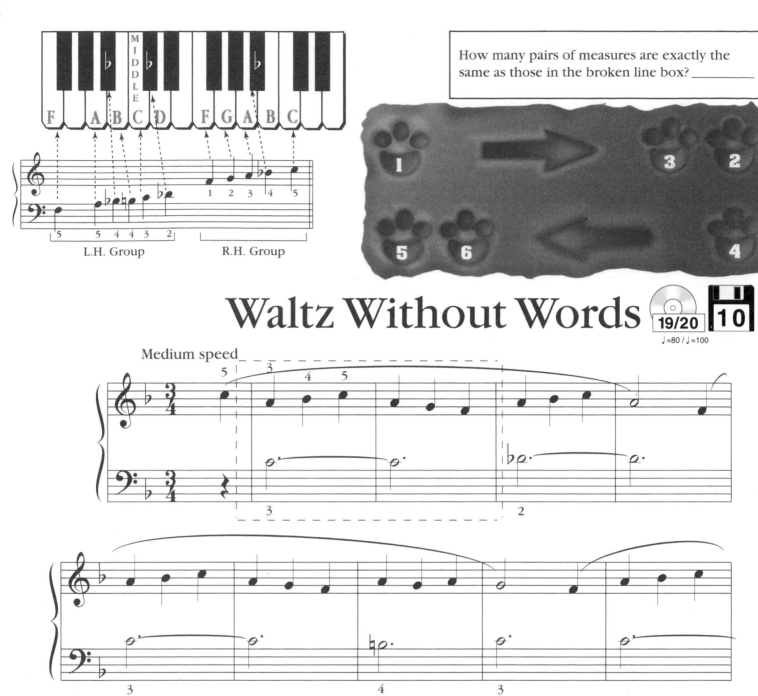

How many pairs of measures are exactly the same as those in the broken line box? _____

Waltz Without Words

19/20 10

♩=80 / ♩=100

Medium speed

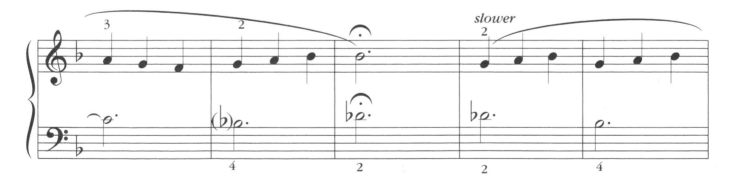

slower

getting slower

PREPARATION: Practice these left hand harmonic intervals:

What does this sign ⌢ mean ?

_____

The New Birthday Song

♩=75 / ♩=95

With authority

medium loud

Hap - py, hap - py   birth - day!

It's a spe - cial   day.   Make a wish, dear   (friend).

L.H. over

Cel - e - brate in ev' - ry   way!
slowing down

11995E

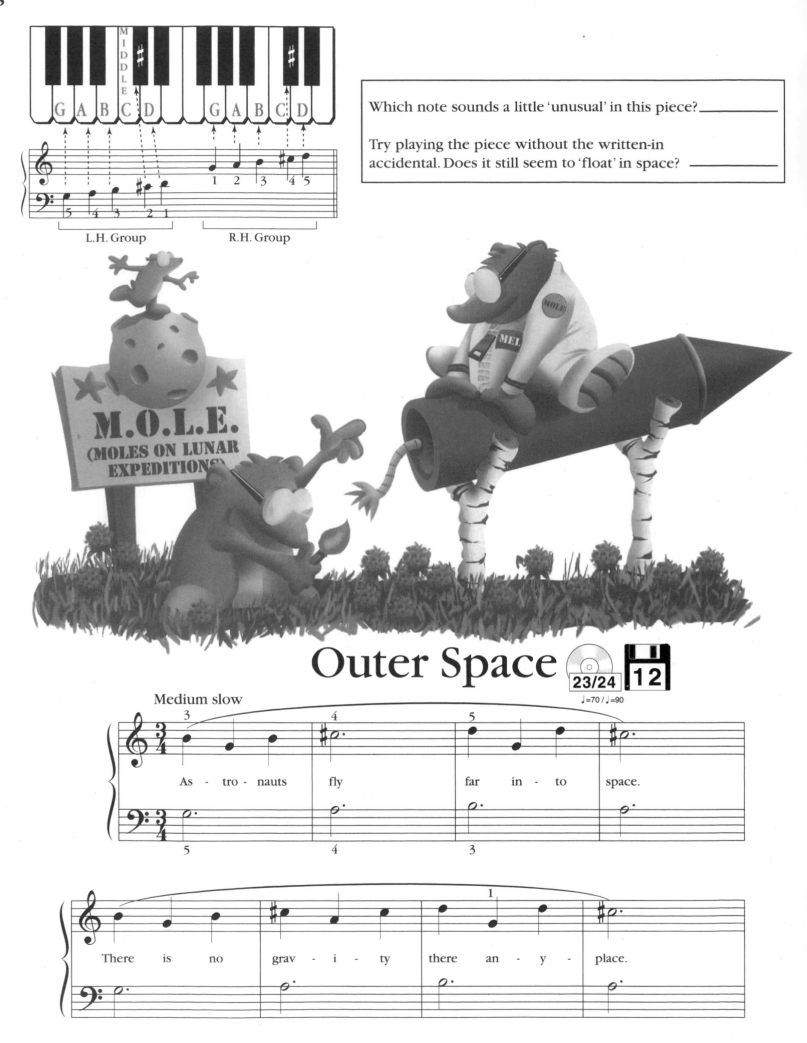

Which note sounds a little 'unusual' in this piece? _____

Try playing the piece without the written-in accidental. Does it still seem to 'float' in space? _____

Outer Space

Medium slow

As - tro - nauts   fly   far   in - to   space.

There   is   no   grav - i - ty   there   an - y - place.

How does it feel walk - ing on air?

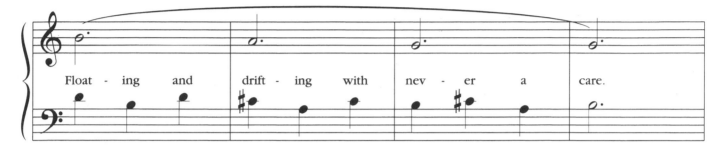

Float - ing and drift - ing with nev - er a care.

slower

What a thing to do! _____

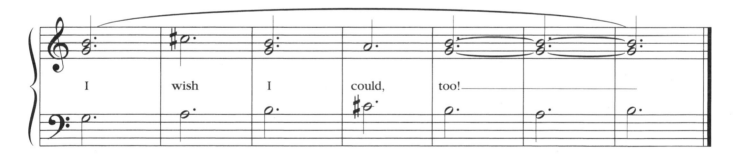

I wish I could, too! _____

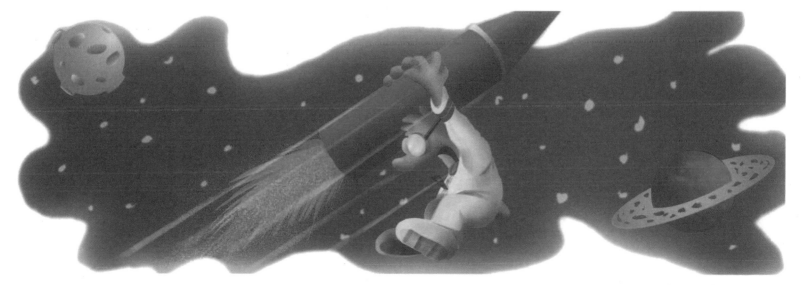

Do you know that B-flat and A-sharp are played on the same black key?
How many A-sharps are in this piece? _____
In which measure does the opening melody return? _____ For how
many measures is it exactly like the beginning? _____

The Circus 25/26 13

♩=105 / ♩=125

did you see a li - on tam - er in the cen - ter

5 3 1 2

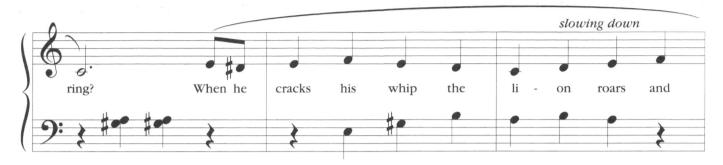

slowing down

ring? When he cracks his whip the li - on roars and

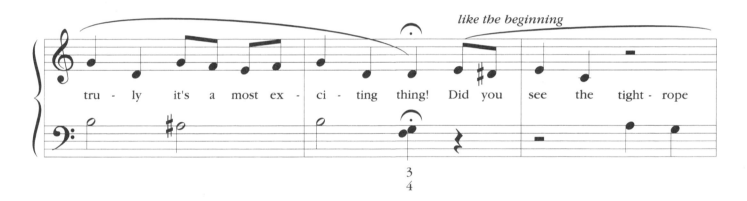

like the beginning

tru - ly it's a most ex - ci - ting thing! Did you see the tight - rope

3
4

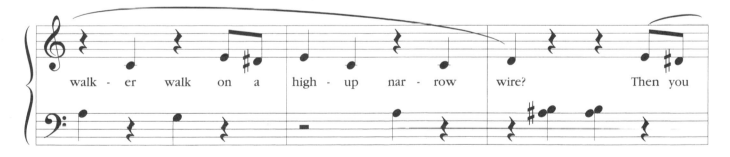

walk - er walk on a high - up nar - row wire? Then you

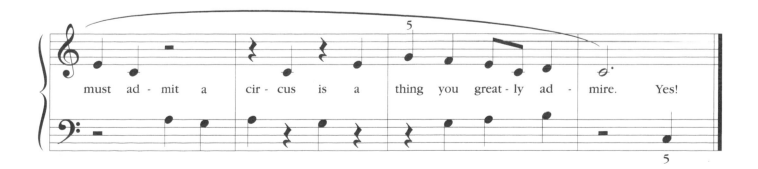

5

must ad - mit a cir - cus is a thing you great - ly ad - mire. Yes!

5

Find the measure where the right hand has three beats
of rest while the left hand has four beats of rest. _____
What note does the key signature tell you to sharp? _____

A Computer ?

27/28   14

♩=95 / ♩=115

Swingingly

medium loud

Have you ev-er seen Grand-ma's writ-ing ma-chine? I

think it is aw-ful-ly old. It clicks and it jumps when I

touch an - y key, but some - thing is miss - ing, I know! It's

hesitatingly

strange - ly fa - mil - iar, but what is - n't there? It's an ob - ject that I've of - ten

getting softer

with confidence

seen. Hmm..... Oh, now I've got it, I

know what it is! A com - put - er with - out an - y screen!

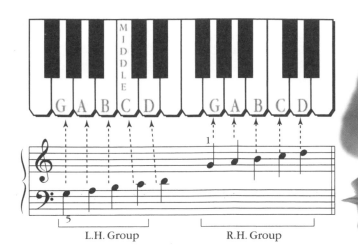

A Coda is a short ending section. Does the Coda in this piece use melodic material from the song? _____ How is it different? What is the name for the two short musical phrases at the beginning? _____

Go Tell Aunt Rhody

29/30 **15**
♩=86 / ♩=106

Medium slow

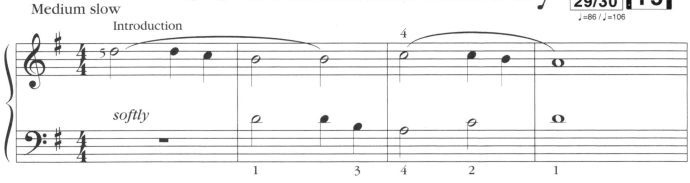

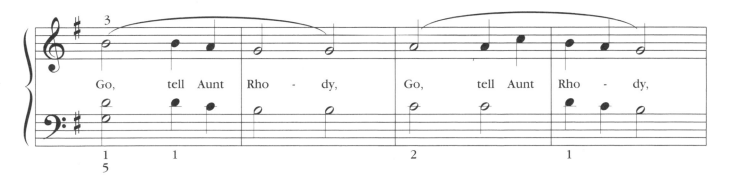

11995E

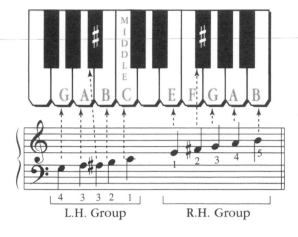

THE MELODY is the part you can sing or hum. In this piece, why do the hands take turns playing the melody?

Two Friends and a Secret

31/32 16

♩=60 / ♩=80

Quietly

With excitement

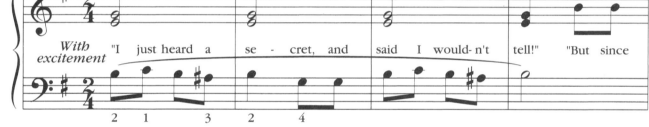

"I just heard a se - cret, and said I would- n't tell!" "But since

I can keep a se - cret, too, you might tell me as well!" "Then just

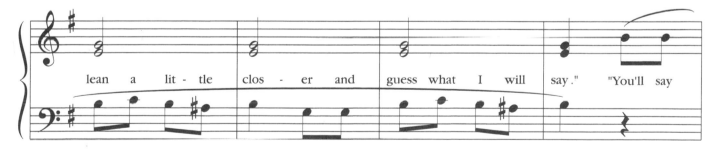

lean a lit - tle clos - er and guess what I will say." "You'll say

ab - so - lute - ly noth - ing, you're not giv - ing it a - way!"

11995E

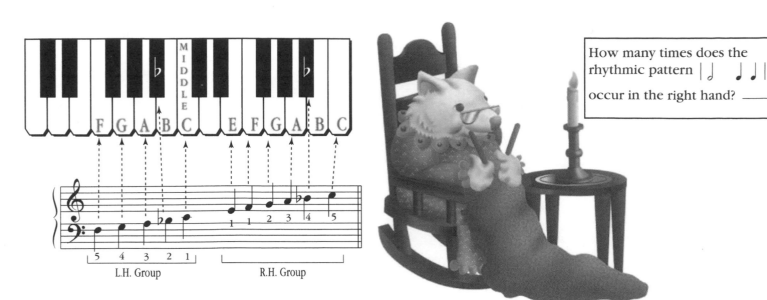

How many times does the rhythmic pattern ♩ ♩♩ occur in the right hand? _____

'Tis A Gift To Be Simple

♩=105 / ♩=125

Kindly

medium loud

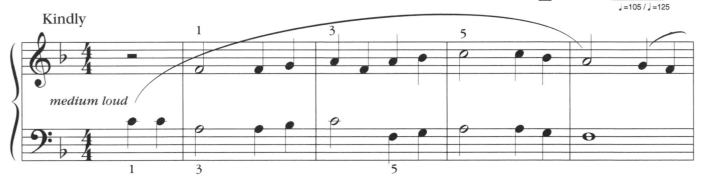

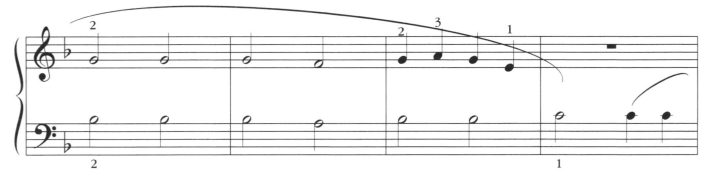

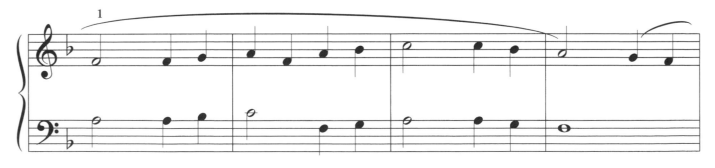

3

Lightly Row

35/36 18
♩=71 / ♩=91

Smoothly
medium soft

Get a boat, find some oars. Then you start out from the shore.

Take your mom or dad with you. They know what to do!

When the wa-ter's ver-y calm row up to a big tall palm.

Rest a-while, soon you'll say, "What a love-ly day!"

11995E

Swanee River
Duet (Secondo)

Stephen Foster

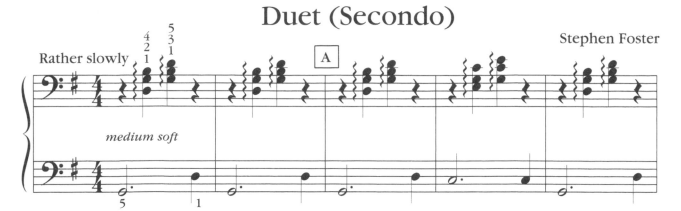

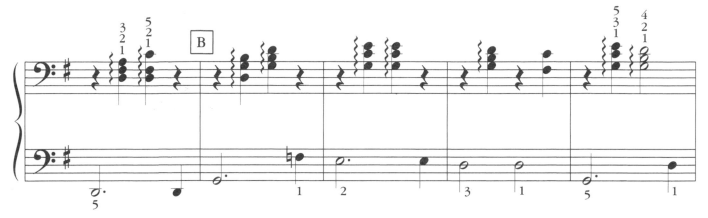

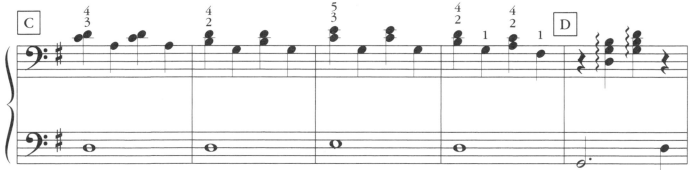

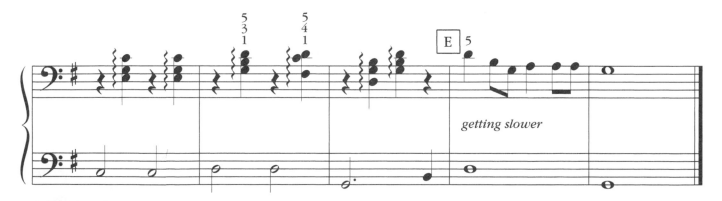

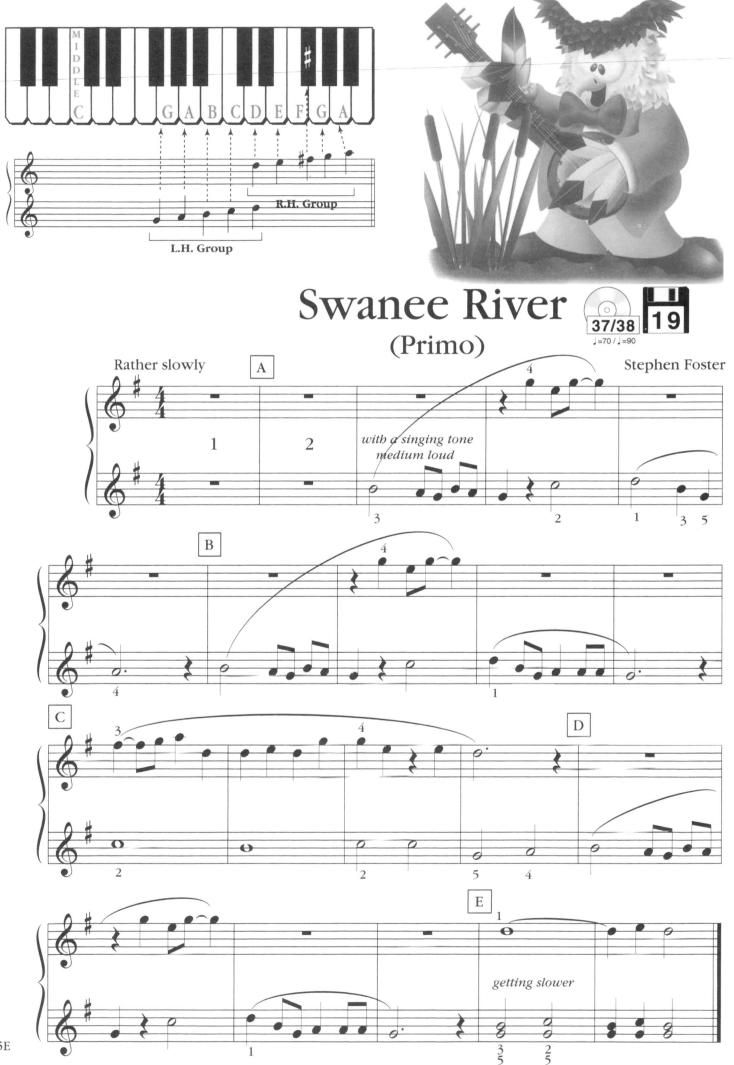

Swanee River
(Primo)

37/38 19

♩=70 / ♩=90

Rather slowly   Stephen Foster

Glossary of Terms and Symbols

TERM	DEFINITION
> Accent	Give extra stress to the note.
Canon	A melody that imitates another. A round.
Coda	A short ending section.
D.C. al Fine	Repeat from the beginning and play to the word "fine".
Eighth Rest	1/2 count of silence.
Fermata	Hold the note for longer than its value.
Fine	The end.
Flat	Play the very closest (usually black) key to the left.
Harmonic Interval	Two keys played together.
Introduction	A short musical phrase before the main part of the piece.
Melody	The part you can hum or sing. Sometimes it has words.
Natural	It cancels a sharp or flat.
Primo	The treble part of a duet.
Secondo	The bass part of a duet.
Sharp	Play the very closest (usually black) key to the right.

CERTIFICATE OF MERIT

This certifies that

has successfully completed

TEACHING LITTLE FINGERS TO PLAY MORE

Teacher

Date

11995E

Leigh Kaplan

Leigh Kaplan began her piano study at the age of eight—her first book being John Thompson's *Teaching Little Fingers to Play*—and holds Baccalaureate and Masters Degrees in Piano Performance from the University of Southern California, where she was a full scholarship recipient.

Ms. Kaplan, who frequently appears as a solo recitalist and ensemble player, has been a guest artist with the Boston Pops and has lectured at universities and on various prestigious platforms, including the Smithsonian Institute. She taught piano at Citrus College in Covina, California, and later served as Assistant Professor of Music at El Camino College in Torrance, California.

Leigh Kaplan's piano solos and piano duets are published by The Willis Music Company, and her classical and jazz recordings are on the Cambria label. She and her husband currently make their home in Arroyo Grande, California.

Nick Gressle

Nick Gressle is a freelance illustrator. He received his Baccalaureate degree in Graphic Design from Northern Kentucky University in 1988, and has since published several of his illustrations in a variety of print and interactive media.

Teaching Little Fingers To Play was Mr. Gressle's first major work for The Willis Music Company.

Mr. Gressle maintains his studio in Mt. Washington, Ohio.